001

002

PLATE 1

BLACK HAWK

"Chief of the Broadleafs"

003

RIP VAN WINKLE

MAY YOU LIVE LONG & PROSPER

004

SHERLOCK HOLMES

SHERLOCK HOLMES

005

ROUND UP

006

VASA

007

WALT. WHITMAN

008

PLATE 2

009

010

Plate 3

011

012

013

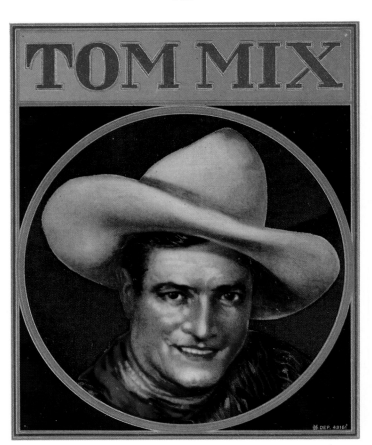

014

PLATE 4

015

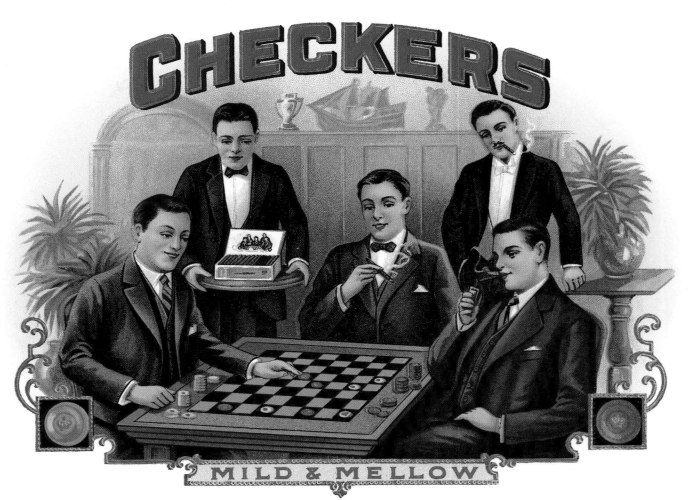

016

PLATE 5

017

018

019

KNOWN TO EVERYONE - LIKED BY ALL

020

"HOLDS YOU UP"

021

022

PLATE 6

023

024

PLATE 7

025

026

027

028

029

PLATE 8

030

031

PLATE 9

032

033

034

035

036

037

PLATE 10

038

039

PLATE 11

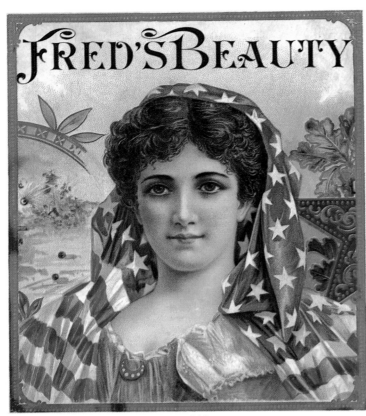

040

041

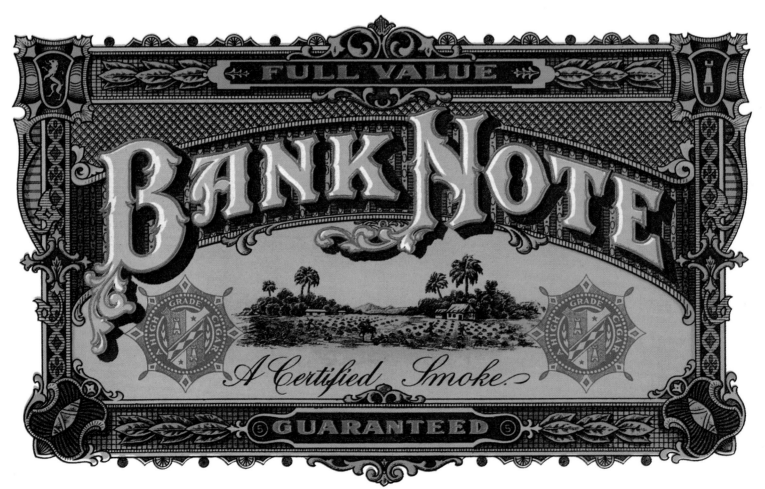

042

PLATE 12

043

044

Plate 13

045

046

047

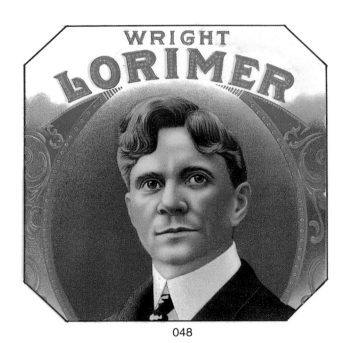

048

049

050

PLATE 14

051

052

PLATE 15

053

054

055

056

057

PLATE 16

058

059

PLATE 17

060

061

062

063

064

065

PLATE 18

LYRA

TITLE AND DESIGN PROPERTY OF AUGUST FREEMAN.   THE CALVERT LITH. CO. DETROIT & CHICAGO.

066

POLITANO

067

PLATE 19

068

069

070

071

072

073

PLATE 20

074

075

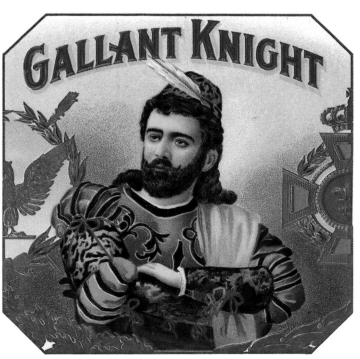

076

PLATE 21

077

078

079

080

081

PLATE 22

082

083

PLATE 23

084

085

086

087

088

089

PLATE 24